SEATTLE
THEN & NOW

SEATTLE
THEN & NOW

JAMES MADISON COLLINS

THUNDER BAY
P·R·E·S·S

Published in the United States by
Thunder Bay Press
5880 Oberlin Drive, San Diego, CA 92121-4794
www.advantagebooksonline.com

Produced by
PRC Publishing Ltd,
8-10 Blenheim Court, Brewery Road,
London N7 9NY

ISBN 1 57145 244 3

Printed and bound in China.

4 5 01 02 03

Collins, James Madison.
Seattle then & now / James Madison Collins.
   p. cm
ISBN 1-57145-244-3
 1. Seattle (Wash.)--Pictorial works. 2. Seattle (Wash.)--History--Pictorial works. 3.
Seattle (Wash.)--Buildings, structures, etc.--Pictorial works. 4. Historic
sites--Washington (State)--Seattle--Pictorial works. I. Title: Seattle then and now. II.
Title.

F899.S443 C64 2000
979.7'72--dc21   00-026906

Acknowledgments
The publisher wishes to thank Simon Clay for taking all the colour photography
in this book, and the Museum of History and Industry, 2700 24th Avenue East,
Seattle, WA 98112, for providing all the black and white photographs, as follows:

PEMCO Webster & Stevens Collection/Museum of History and Industry, Seattle,
WA for the front cover and pages 1, 6, 8, 10, 12, 14, 18, 20, 22, 26, 28, 30, 32, 34,
36, 38, 40, 42, 44, 46, 48, 50, 52, 54, 56, 58, 60, 62, 64, 66, 68, 70, 72, 74, 76, 78, 80,
82, 86, 88, 90, 92, 94, 98, 102, 104, 106, 112, 114, 116, 118, 120, 124, 126, 128, 130,
134, 136 (main and inset), 138

Museum of History and Industry, Seattle, WA for pages 16, 24, 84, 96, 100, 108,
110, 122, 132, 142

Seattle Post-Intelligencer Collection/Museum of History and Industry, Seattle, WA
for page 140

Back cover: Simon Clay

INTRODUCTION

Seattle is a city of change. Sometimes radical, sometimes gradual, but always at its core lies the spirit and force of constant evolution. That change has marked the progress of both the city and the world—widely felt in the circles of engineering, economics, culture, and technology. Despite its relative youth, the "Emerald City" enters the 21st century as one of the most influential urban centers on the planet.

Its beginnings were inauspicious, a settlement founded in 1851 on a point of land jutting into Puget Sound, surrounded by rugged mountains and daunting bodies of fresh and salt water. Eventually the population center shifted from what was known as Alki Point, now part of West Seattle, toward the eastern shore of Elliott Bay. There the town grew around the commercial center of today's Pioneer Square, relying on the timber industry for its livelihood. Much of the original downtown area, roughly 60 square blocks, was wiped out by the devastating fire of 1889. But that blaze, which could have signaled the end of the fledgling city, instead served as a harbinger of change. As Seattle rebuilt its business core from the ashes, important developments were approaching.

Two major events, just a few years apart, radically altered Seattle's fortunes near the close of the 1800s. The completion of the Great Northern Railroad in 1893, followed soon after by the discovery of gold in Alaska's Klondike territory, unleashed a torrent of prosperity upon the city, a happy coincidence that sparked explosive expansion around the turn of the 20th century. Even the struggle against nature, which included flattening hills, building bridges, digging canals, and raising the streets of downtown to prevent the city's flush toilets from exploding during high tide, could not deter Seattle's growth. Smith Tower, completed in 1914, rose 500 feet above its foundation and long ranked as the tallest building west of the Mississippi River.

The Great Depression ground the expansion to a halt in the 1920s and 1930s. But the kernel of recovery had already been planted by a small airplane company with a factory south of downtown, and the onset of World War II would make Boeing a household name in aviation. The company's giant four-engine bombers emerged as symbols of American innovation and industrial capability, and by the end of the war, Seattle had found another economic foundation to fill the void left by the Depression. As jet-powered commercial aviation boomed in the post-war era, Boeing would become the single most important aircraft manufacturer in the world. One of the early prototypes of the famed 707 model, put through a series of astonishing aerobatics by company test pilot "Tex" Johnston in full view of the spectators of the 1955 Seafair hydroplane races on Lake Washington, earned Seattle the moniker of "Jet City." Boeing would eventually expand to the neighboring towns of Everett and Renton; today it employs more than 100,000 people in the greater Seattle metropolitan area. Since its recent merger with erstwhile rival McDonnell Douglas, Boeing ranks as the globe's largest aerospace firm and one of the 40 largest international corporations overall.

Even as Boeing was growing, technology would take Seattle in another direction. The information revolution built momentum in the 1970s and 1980s, eventually catapulting a locally based software company to incredible heights. Microsoft would establish its world headquarters in Redmond, across Lake Washington from Seattle, but the rise of computer-related business would grow to rival Boeing in importance to the area's economy. At the end of the century, nearly 700 high-tech companies are located in Seattle and its suburbs. The commercial promise of the Internet has only added to the prosperity, with the prospect of even greater success ahead.

While its economy evolved, the city itself underwent a long series of physical changes. Freeways, floating bridges, and ferries connected the central urban core to a wide range of outlying towns. With the benefits of that transportation network, though, came a downside: the beginning of traffic congestion that remains Seattle's most pressing issue. The addition of a major international airport and the continued development of the shipping industry, both linking the city to ports of call around the world, had tremendous tangible impact upon both the landscape and the economy. The last quarter-century has brought on an avalanche of construction projects in downtown, largely wiping away the older buildings and replacing them with massive skyscrapers. From the boxy, utilitarian creations of the 1960s and 1970s to the far more elegant glass and steel creations of the 1980s and 1990s, Seattle's skyline is dominated by the visions of modern architects. Still, the residents strive to maintain a reasonable balance between urban sprawl and the environment. Where nature's obstacles were once viewed as something to be vanquished, Seattle's more recent emphasis on a harmonious relationship with the land and water has produced one of the world's greenest cities, surrounded by astounding natural beauty.

As a cultural center, Seattle made a significant stride forward in 1962 when it hosted the World Exposition. Its most lasting contribution, perhaps, was structural: the famous Space Needle became an instantly recognizable symbol. But the Expo was also a sign that Seattle had grown enough in importance to claim a place on the world stage, that it was developing into a truly international city. Immigrants from the Pacific Rim flooded to the area, creating a rich diversity that remains one of Seattle's trademarks. The city's influence was also felt in the spheres of art and music, from the glass-blown works of Dale Chihuly to the searing psychedelic guitar of rock virtuoso Jimi Hendrix. Later, the so-called "grunge rock" scene took root in the Pacific Northwest, sparking another music revolution late in the 1980s.

Nearing its 150th anniversary, Seattle is a city with history and character, but one that is still truly searching for its own unique identity. A result of its evolving nature and great socioeconomic diversity is the inevitable lack of a single, universally recognized defining feature. In spite of that struggle, however, Seattle remains poised at the forefront of the global scene, propelled there by its myriad contributions to the modern world.

James Madison Collins

Webster & Stevens made copies of the work of a number of earlier Seattle photographers. Some of their photos, like this one, show what Seattle looked like a few years before the great fire of 1889. Taken around 1886, it shows Budlong's Boathouse on Front Street (now First Avenue) at the foot of Marion Street. The sailboats and other small watercraft that crowd the waterfront were for rent. The large building in the center is the Frye Opera House, considered the grandest stage north of San Francisco. Almost all of the buildings in this photo would burn in the fire.

A portion of Seattle's waterfront and downtown skyline at dusk. Bank of America Tower, at left center, is a prime example of both the city's skyscraper boom in the 1980s and the havoc wreaked upon the names of such landmarks by the vagaries of modern finance. Originally named Columbia Seafirst Center, it was renamed in 1999 when Seafirst Bank merged with Bank of America.

Before a regular ferry service operated, hundreds of small steamers competed to carry people and freight around Puget Sound. There were so many of these vessels making short runs between so many towns and islands, that they were called the "Mosquito Fleet." In this 1915 photo, the steamer *Iroquois* pulls in to Colman Dock in Seattle. The *Iroquois* was one of the larger steamers and ran between Seattle and Victoria, British Columbia. Smith Tower rises in the background, to the right of the clock tower on Colman Dock.

Smith Tower dominates the cityscape immediately behind Colman Dock in this view. The Washington State ferry system is the nation's most extensive, with commuters relying heavily on both the vehicle and passenger ferries to connect Seattle with the islands of Puget Sound and the cities of Bremerton, Washington, and Vancouver, British Columbia.

By the end of the 1920s, Seattle's waterfront was crowded with docks and its skyline was getting taller. This photo, taken from Colman Dock around 1931, is part of a panoramic view of the city. The tallest landmarks are the Exchange Building (left) and Smith Tower (right).

View from the large parking area at Colman Dock, with the Federal Building and Wells Fargo Center on the left, Bank of America Tower partially obscuring Key Tower at center, and Smith Tower on the right. At 943 feet, the Bank of America Tower, completed in 1985, is the second tallest building on the West Coast; only the First Interstate World Center in Los Angeles is taller.

Left: The ferry *Kalakala* began service in 1935 when its streamlined design immediately made it internationally famous and popular with visitors and residents alike. The ferry made six daily runs between Seattle and Bremerton, and made summer evening excursions around Puget Sound. Unfortunately it vibrated badly and it was also difficult to handle and expensive to repair. Consequently, service ended in 1967 and the ferry became a shore-based seafood processing plant in Alaska. During the 1990s, however, a group of devoted *Kalakala* fans dug the old ferry out of the gravel and returned it to Seattle. This 1935 photo shows the *Kalakala* on a run along the Seattle waterfront. The ferry's name means "flying bird" in the Chinook trade language used by traders and Puget Sound native peoples.

Right: A view of the waterfront and downtown today. The Smith Tower still stands out on the right, with the Bank of America Tower (center) partially concealing Key Tower, and the Henry M. Jackson Federal Building (left) obscuring most of Wells Fargo Center. Efforts are underway to restore *Kalakala*, now berthed on Lake Union, and to find a permanent home for her somewhere along the waterfront, moored as a floating shopping and conference center.

In this busy scene shoppers with their baskets hurry around the Corner Market at Pike Place or stop to chat. An automobile waits while a wagon rushes past, and a streetcar stops at the corner. Seattle opened its public market at Pike Place in 1907 so that farmers could sell fresh eggs, dairy products, produce, and other goods directly to city dwellers. The Corner Market was built several years later across the street at the corner of First Avenue and Pike Place.

Even with its tremendous popularity as a tourist attraction, the Public Market is still, above all, a center of commerce. Shops and street vendors fill the market facility itself and crowd Pike Place, which runs north from Pike Street along the east side of the main building. Ground level from this vantage point is actually the top of the market; it drops several floors to meet Western Avenue on the west side of the structure.

It seems as if Seattle has always had traffic jams at the corner of First Avenue and Pike Street, as this 1919 photo attests. Streetcars can be seen traveling along the brick-paved avenue in both directions and a line of cars is headed south. The traffic waits at the corner while pedestrians cross the streets on their way to the Pike Place Market. The large Statue of Liberty marks the Liberty Theater, where patrons could leave their groceries in a check-room during the show.

Looking northwest along First Avenue at the same intersection. Note the difference in the construction of the roads, with First using conventional pavement and Pike Street at this junction made up of smoothed bricks. Other streets near the Public Market, including Pike Place, also make heavy use of bricks.

In this 1920 photo, grocery store trucks and automobiles crowd Pike Place between the market buildings. Shoppers hurry across the cobblestones, leaving blurs in the photograph. In the early days of the Pike Place Market, all produce was brought to market by horse and wagon and farmers had to get up well before dawn to make sure they got a prime selling position. By 1920, however, motorized trucks and cars had replaced most of the old delivery wagons, making the trip shorter and easier for both farmers and shoppers.

A direct view down Pike Street, across First Avenue, and into the heart of the Public Market, with its famous red sign and clock. The overhead wires provide power to city buses, many of which are equipped to use electric propulsion in available areas and conventional engines elsewhere, part of an effort to reduce pollution in the urban center.

By 1908, Seattle's Second Avenue looked much as it does today. The city had removed part of Denny Hill, and businessmen had replaced the old hilltop Washington Hotel with a building at the lower street level. The old Washington Hotel had stood at the level of the roof of the theater. Visitors to the city also admired the new ornamental streetlights that had begun to line the main business streets.

In this photo, pedestrians cross Pine Street, while wagon traffic moves along Second Avenue past the new electric streetlights. The new Washington Hotel (now The Josephinum) is the large building at the center, behind the wagon, and the Moore Theatre is just beyond it.

The intersection of Second and Pine today, between Pike Place Public Market (to the west) and Westlake Center (to the east). The Josephinum and the Moore Theater are visible at center, with an office building on the left and a multi-level parking structure to the right. Many of Seattle's older buildings have long since been replaced by parking facilities, an inevitable result of urban congestion.

After the University of Washington moved to its present campus it put together a master plan for the development of its downtown Seattle property. The plan included office buildings, a theater, a hotel, and stores. The White and Henry Buildings are two of three connected office buildings built along Fourth Avenue as part of this plan. This photo shows the White and Henry Buildings from the corner of Union Street and Fourth Avenue. In 1974, the buildings were torn down to make room for Rainier Square.

A view of one corner of Rainier Square from the intersection of Fourth and Union. In the background looms Rainier Tower, with the top portion of its unusual funnel-shaped base just visible. This strange-looking foundation, much narrower at ground level than at its junction with the bulk of the building, gives Rainier Tower the appearance of rather precarious stability.

This photo shows the Brooklyn Block sometime between 1897 and 1900. A café and cigar store occupy the ground floor at Second Avenue, and an upholsterer and plumber and other small businesses all have entryways off the wooden sidewalk that runs along University Street, at the side of the building.

A clear vision of the sharp contrast in 100 years of building design. Now the Brooklyn stands in the shadow of one of Seattle's steel and glass monsters, the Washington Mutual Tower. Only the lower portion of this 730-foot skyscraper is visible in this photo; it ranks as the third-tallest building in the city.

A view of the wooden catwalks and scaffolding used during construction of the Olympic Hotel at Fourth Avenue and University Street in downtown Seattle. The Olympic Hotel was built from steel, brick, concrete, and terra cotta. Like many taller city buildings the decoration on the lower floors is much more detailed than that on the upper floors. The elegance of the lower floors was meant to attract people at street level.

Like the nearby Fifth Avenue Theatre, the Four Seasons Olympic Hotel today conveys a sense of glamour and prestige that more modern structures often lack. Even with the growth of the downtown area and the construction of high-rise hotels, the Olympic still sets the city's standard for luxurious accommodation.

This photo was taken around the time of the 1926 opening of the Fifth Avenue Theatre. It shows the brightly decorated floors, doors, and ceiling of the theater's lobby. Audiences were fascinated with the decor of the new theater. Its brightly-painted woodwork had been inspired by traditional Chinese decorated wood structures in Beijing's Forbidden City. The Asian theme was in keeping with Seattle's position as a gateway for Pacific trade.

The colorful exterior of the Fifth Avenue Theatre's lobby today. Much painstaking care has been taken to keep the facility's unique design in top condition, as the Fifth Avenue Theatre remains one of Seattle's premiere venues for the performing arts, and a vivid reminder of the city's history.

Left: This photo shows the Coliseum Theater in 1934 when its large domed entry canopy was still standing. The theater, at the northeast corner of Fifth Avenue and Pike Street, was the world's first hall designed just for the movies. Unlike other theaters of its time it had no stage for live acts. It did, however, have a nursery for children and an organ and orchestra to play along with silent movies.

Right: The theater today, a refreshingly archaic sight in the midst of one of downtown's most modern areas. Its conversion to a retail store seems a small price to pay to retain its elegant features, thus saving it from the fate of so many of its contemporaries. Visible behind it is 520 Pike Tower, a 29-floor structure that stands nearly 500 feet.

Frederick & Nelson was one of Seattle's landmark companies for over a century. The first Frederick & Nelson retail store opened in 1889, right after Seattle's great fire, and by 1916 the company was doing so well that it built a large new store at Fifth Avenue and Pike Street, which many people thought was too far out of town. This photo shows that store shortly after it opened.

Though Frederick & Nelson did not survive as a company, the building, with four floors added over the years, soldiers on. Purchased by Nordstrom, a Fortune 500 Seattle-based retailer, and extensively refurbished, the structure reopened in 1998 as the flagship store for its new owners and a centerpiece for the revitalization of the downtown shopping area.

Spotlights shine on the front of the building, as a crowd gathers for the opening night of the Fifth Avenue Theatre on September 24, 1926. It was located between Union and University Streets and featured movies and performing acts. Admission to the opening was 65 cents for adults and 25 cents for children

This corner of Second and Union is now home to a parking garage, recently built to help support the seemingly endless waves of vehicle traffic that crowd the downtown streets. The very top of U.S. Bank Center, one of the city's newest skyscrapers, is visible in the right background.

In 1913, Seattleites looking west from the top of the stairway from Fourth Avenue to Yesler Way would have seen several new buildings. Most eye-catching was the almost-complete Smith Tower, then the tallest building west of the Mississippi River. In this photo, taken around 1913, the new Hotel Seward can be seen at the base of Smith Tower, and the Frye Hotel stands to the left, across Yesler. In 1914 ground would be broken for Seattle's new County-City Building on the site of the Coliseum Theater.

A somewhat more distant view of Smith Tower and the Frye Building, with most of the
tower obscured by foliage. At an even 500 feet, it remained Seattle's tallest structure
until the construction of the 605-foot Space Needle in 1962, and was not supplanted as
the city's tallest building until the rise of the 609-foot skyscraper at 1001 Fourth
Avenue in 1969.

The Smith Tower was Seattle's first skyscraper. When it opened in 1914, it was described as the "monster structure (that) acts as a guiding beacon to vessels in and out of Elliott Bay." Indeed, for many years it was the tallest building west of the Mississippi. The photo shows the Smith Tower dwarfing an earlier landmark, the Hotel Seattle. The triangular hotel building, which was built less than 20 years before Smith Tower, was located near the corner of First Avenue and Yesler Way.

Though no longer qualifying as such a "monster structure," at least not by modern standards, Smith Tower remains a proud symbol of the city's early expansion, fueled largely by profits derived from Seattle's important role in opening the Alaskan frontier to gold prospectors at the turn of the 20th century.

In about 1912 a group of citizens pushed for a new governmental "Civic Center" in the recently regraded Denny Hill area. This effort failed, but four years later their efforts were rewarded when the new King County Courthouse and Municipal Building, also known as the County-City Building, opened on Third Avenue, convenient to the heart of the old downtown. Dating from around 1921, the photo shows the County-City Building, with Smith Tower in the background.

A contemporary view of Smith Tower and the County-City Building, with the blue waters of Elliott Bay and the rugged mountains of the Olympic Peninsula, across Puget Sound, just visible at lower left. Some of the city's administrative departments are now housed in the Key Tower skyscraper on the corner of Fifth Avenue and Columbia.

Left: In the early 1900s Westlake Avenue ran from Lake Union through what is now Westlake Park in downtown Seattle. Fourth Avenue ran up a steep hill, but it was later regraded to the same level as Westlake. The Plaza Hotel stood at the intersection of Fourth Avenue and Westlake and is shown in this photo, probably taken in 1909. There were a few automobiles at that time, but the scene is busy with pedestrians, carts, wagons, and streetcars. An oyster bar, a café, several hotels, and other businesses line the streets. Canvas awnings shade the sidewalk, and two street vendors are sheltered by Bon Marche umbrellas.

Right: The view across Westlake Park, south of Westlake Center, looking south along Fourth Avenue. The 30-floor Century Square building stands at right, with the Washington Mutual Tower in the right background and the top of Rainier Tower just visible in the left background. Pine Street, in the foreground, was closed off to vehicle traffic between Fourth and Fifth Avenues until two years ago.

Inset: Photo taken from the center of Westlake Park looking north, with Westlake Center Office Tower (center) rising above the four-level shopping area at its base. The metal arch at left is one of the variety of ornamental structures that dot the park, which has become a popular staging area for civic events and public rallies.

Some of Seattle's steep streets had cable cars that moved by gripping a long wire cable that ran under the street; when the cars needed to stop they simply released the grip. This photo was taken on James Street in 1905—when it still had wooden sidewalks—looking downhill toward Pioneer Square. The cross street at the bottom of the slope is Second Avenue.

The same view today, taken from the intersection of Third Avenue and James Street. The artificial elevation of the street level in area around Pioneer Square since the original photo was taken is clearly evident from the reduced grade of James Street. The cable cars and their tracks have disappeared into history, replaced by buses as Seattle's primary mass transit system.

A particularly good overall view of Pioneer Square in about 1910. Streetcars move along the brick streets, and people wait for their rides under the glass-covered pergola. By the time this photo was taken the central business district had begun to move northward, but before about 1905 Pioneer Square was the heart of Seattle's central business district. Large brick buildings were built after the 1889 fire and the square was the start of many of the city's streetcar lines.

Pioneer Square today, with the Smith Tower visible on the right. Much of the area around the square is elevated from 8 to 35 feet above the original street level, the result of the need for an improved sewage system to compensate for the city's proximity to Elliott Bay, and the adverse effect of high tide on the flush toilet system at the turn of the century.

Left: The totem pole at Pioneer Square has been a Seattle landmark since 1899. In that year, a group of Seattle businessmen visited the Tlingit village of Tongrass, in Alaska. They thought the village was deserted, removed the 50-foot tall pole as a souvenir, transported it back to Seattle, and had it set up in the square. They were later fined for the theft. Created as a memorial to a woman of the Raven Clan, the pole was replaced in 1938 by a duplicate carved by Tlingit craftsmen after rot and fire damaged the original.

Right: The second pole today, with a close-up of the images at its base, at the north end of Pioneer Square. The square also includes a visitor center for the Klondike Gold Rush National Historical Park; most of the park is located in Alaska, administering trails that lead to the gold fields of the Klondike.

Between 1800 and 1884 Seattle's population grew from 3,533 to 12,632, and the city accordingly spent $250,000 on street improvements. New businesses along Front Street near Madison and Spring Streets included the Frye Opera House, a market, a drug store, and a boot and shoe store. A nearby stationery store also sold books, magazines, and wallpaper. This is the view from the opera house around 1885, showing a scene of the growing city.

Traffic flows both directions along First Avenue today, one of the few north–south streets through this part of downtown that remains a two-way thoroughfare. Most of the numbered avenues, and many of the cross-streets, are designated as one-way roads. As a result, navigating downtown Seattle can be a daunting experience for visitors.

In the 1880s, when Seattle's business district was near Pioneer Square, loggers, miners, and others came to this part of the city to find work, supplies, and entertainment. Others came to Seattle to attend the Territorial University, which stood on a hill above the city. This photo, taken around 1884, shows the intersection of Commercial Street (now First Avenue South) and Main Street, looking north toward Mill Street (now Yesler Way). The University of the Territory of Washington is in the center distance.

Today the area around Pioneer Square is more noted for its nightlife and tourism than its business functions. The roads running toward the water through this section of downtown were the origin for the term "skid row"—originally, timber logs were skidded down the slopes of the hill toward the waterfront as a convenient method of moving them. This practice led to the phrase "skid road," which was later modified.

Seattle's Front and Madison Streets recovered quickly after the great fire of 1889 and by 1891 the shoe store, restaurant, and other businesses seen here were occupying new brick buildings. This is a bustling scene of a city finding its feet after a major disaster. Streetcars run along Front Street's (now called First Avenue) trestle and cable cars climb Madison's steep hills. Billboards advertise business investments and Levi clothing. The towers of Providence Hospital (left) and Central School (center) rise in the distance.

The original brick structure at left center now houses a sporting goods store, but most of its contemporaries have vanished, replaced by skyscrapers, four of which are clearly visible in this photo. From left to right are 1000 Second Avenue, 1001 Fourth Place, Wells Fargo Center, and the Henry M. Jackson Federal Building.

This photo—looking south along First Avenue—was taken around 1907 at a time when Seattle's downtown was booming. The area near University Street is lined with hotels and other businesses, and streetcars move along the center of the avenue, while carts and wagons drive nearer the curb. The darker streetcar is headed north to Ballard Beach and the lighter one carries the mail.

The Alaska Building today, a legacy of gold fever that swept through Seattle when vast quantities of that most valuable of metals were discovered in the Klondike territory in 1897. Still well-used as an office building, the Alaska stands in the shadow of the Smith Tower, partially visible to the right.

During World War I banks sold government bonds to raise money for the war effort. In this 1917 photo, a man reads the war bond poster outside the Seattle National Bank, at the corner of Second Avenue and Columbia Street.

The Seattle National Bank building still stands at the intersection of Columbia Street and Second Avenue; now the imposing gray walls, built to protect the cash and precious metals of a city experiencing an economic boom after the Klondike Gold Rush, house a fitness center appropriately named "The Vault."

Seattle's First Methodist Episcopal Church stood at the corner of Third Avenue and Marion Street. It was torn down in 1908 when Third Avenue was regraded and the congregation then built a new building—First Methodist Church, further up Marion Street, at Fifth Avenue. This 1905 photo of Seattle's First Methodist Episcopal Church gives a good idea of the original building's Victorian Gothic architecture.

The radical changes in Seattle's architecture are readily apparent, comparing the original church with the "modern" office building that replaced it, and that structure with the high-rises behind it. From left to right are the Fifth Avenue Plaza, Key Tower, Bank of America Tower, and the Pacific Building.

Left: This photo was taken between 1903 and 1907, a time when Third Avenue was lined with homes as well as businesses. Plymouth Congregational Church (right) stood at the corner of Third Avenue and University Street and the Washington Hotel, seen at the far end of Third Avenue (center), dominated Denny Hill. By 1907 the hotel and much of the hill had been removed in regrading projects.

Right: Third Avenue today, flanked by a mix of old and new construction. Under the street is the main line for the city's underground bus tunnel, used to complement the bus lines on the surface roads. Passengers can access it at six points along its route; its limited length, though, means the tunnel will remain something of a novelty rather than developing into the basis for a truly effective mass transit system.

In 1890 Seattle City Hall moved into King County's old courthouse at Third Avenue and Jefferson Street. Seattle's population grew very fast during the next 18 years and as the city boomed the city government kept adding onto the old building. It eventually looked so strange that people nicknamed it the "Katzenjammer Castle" after a popular comic strip of the time. This is a photo of Seattle's old city hall building in about 1911. The original courthouse building is to the left in the photograph.

A few blocks away, the County-City Building, eventual replacement for the old court-house and city hall, seen today. The two distinct stages of construction are clearly visible even now, with the original lower floors differing in appearance from the upper levels. City government gradually outgrew this structure as well.

Seattle's fire department headquarters in 1911, with firemen, fire engines, and the chief's wagon standing in the doorways. The city's original two main fire stations were burned to the ground during the great fire of 1889 and the department subsequently built a new brick headquarters on Columbia Street between Sixth and Seventh Avenues. The department also replaced its volunteer firemen with professionals, upgraded the alarm system, and bought new fire-fighting equipment.

The construction of Interstate Five greatly altered the western slope of First Hill above downtown. Most notably visible in this view are the Fifth Avenue Plaza (left), the Madison Renaissance Hotel (left center), and the skyscrapers of One and Two Union Square (far right). Two Union Square, completed in 1989, stands nearly 300 feet higher than its 1981 counterpart.

King County Court House

Left: In 1890 King County's courts moved into a new courthouse that had been built at Seventh Avenue and Jefferson Street, far above downtown Seattle. The hill soon became known as "Profanity Hill" due to the swearing done by people who had to make the steep climb, but its tall dome could be seen for miles, and it appears in many old photographs of Seattle. The courts moved downhill again in 1917, this time to a new building on Third Avenue, and the old Courthouse was torn down in the 1930s. This photo shows the King County Courthouse in about 1903.

Above: One symbol of justice and law enforcement replaced by another, as a Seattle police cruiser sits poised very near where the old courthouse once stood. The original site of the courthouse is now buried underneath the wide lanes of Interstate Five. James Street, one block to the north, runs under the freeway, but Jefferson Street has been divided.

In Seattle and other larger U.S. cities there were often several stations where different railroad lines stopped for passengers and freight. Several lines stopped at the Oregon−Washington Station and the building, now called Union Station, still stands at Fourth Avenue and Jackson Street.

Union Station today, viewed from the northwest, with construction of the
new 505 Union Station office building evident behind the original structure.
On the east side of Union Station is the southern terminal for Seattle's
underground bus tunnel, which runs northwest, following Third Avenue
before turning northeast at Pine Street and ending north of the Convention
Center.

Seattle's first railway station stood near where King Street Station stands today. At that time much of the land in that part of the city was still underwater at high tide, and the tracks of the Columbia & Puget Sound Railroad ran over the tidelands on wooden trestles. Taken about 1880, this photo shows the depot and railroad tracks.

The clock tower of King Street Station flanked by construction in the International District (left) and the distinctive shape of the Kingdome roof (right). Built in 1975, the 66,000-seat indoor stadium was once the home of Seattle's professional football, baseball, and basketball teams. The ubiquitous structure will soon disappear from the skyline; it is scheduled for demolition in April 2000.

During the hard times of the 1930s' economic depression, many unemployed and homeless people settled just west of where Seattle's Kingdome now stands. They built ramshackle houses out of scrap material and elected their own mayor. The area was nicknamed "Hooverville" or "Hoover City" by people who blamed President Herbert Hoover for causing the Great Depression. This 1933 photo shows the small houses of "Hooverville" scattered between the roadway and the waterfront.

The Alaskan Way viaduct (right), a two-level elevated roadway that supports Highway 99, streams past stacked cargo containers south of downtown. To the north and west lie the piers of Seattle's industrial shipyards, built around the banks and mouth of the Duwamish River where it meets Elliott Bay. Highway 99 was the region's major north–south vehicle route before the construction of Interstate Five.

The Seattle Brewing & Malting Company was founded in 1878 and built its large Bayview Brewery in 1890. Several years later, the company merged with a firm that eventually became today's Rainier Brewing Company. Dating from around 1915, the photo shows the company's Bayview Brewery Buildings. Some of these buildings are still in use and can be seen from Interstate Five, just south of downtown Seattle.

Destined forever to be known as "The Brewery," the building has now been sold and put into use by a coffee company. Though Rainier Beer is no longer made here, the brightly lit red "R" atop the structure will remain in place. After the sale of the brewery, there was considerable public outcry over the potential fate of the popular symbol. The new ownership agreed to keep the "R" in its original place.

Left: This photo shows how the Georgetown City Hall building looked in the mid-1920s. Georgetown, located to the north of Boeing Field, was once a separate city connected to Seattle by streetcar. It became part of Seattle in 1910. In the 1920s, Georgetown sold its city hall, though it remained a center of community activity. It housed a baby clinic, the police department, and a branch of the Seattle Public Library.

Right: Georgetown City Hall survives, but the town itself has lost most of its identity as a residential neighborhood. The area north of Boeing Field and south of downtown has become largely industrial, with Beacon Hill to the east becoming much more heavily populated over the years.

This photo, taken in June 1917, shows the new factory, Plant 1, of the Boeing Airplane Company, which was built after Boeing got its first big military order when its "C" model seaplane was accepted as a trainer by the U.S. Navy during World War I. The company opened the new plant on the west side of the Duwamish River, south of Seattle, to handle the increased business.

Now part of the massive Boeing Field complex south of downtown, the original building stands as a reminder of the aerospace giant's humble origins. Boeing built its reputation with the performance of its B-17 and B-29 bombers during World War II, and emerged as a driving force behind the postwar boom in jet-powered commercial aviation.

Looking south toward the tower of Seattle's King Street Station, taken from Smith Tower sometime around 1929, near the center of the picture Second Avenue continues south, splitting into Second Avenue South Extensions (left) and Second Avenue South (right). The streets have been hung with flags for a Shriners' event.

Modern street-level view of the split of Second Avenue, with the Metropolis Building on the right and the north side of the Frye Building, now converted from a hotel to apartments, on the left. The clock tower of King Street Station is just visible in the center background.

Left: In 1909 sculptor James Wehn designed three fountains with the bust of Chief Seattle. One was placed at Pioneer Square, another on Occidental Street, and a third at the intersection of Fourth and Westlake Avenues. The fountains were designed to provide water for people, horses, and dogs. This is the fountain at the intersection of Fourth and Westlake Avenues in about 1925.

Right: The lone surviving fountain of the original three still pumps out water on the southern edge of Pioneer Square, one of a handful of reminders of the contributions of the original inhabitants of the area. The name "Seattle" is an English approximation of *Sealth*, though the original form can also be frequently found in the local terminology.

The Times Square Building was the headquarters of the *Seattle Times* as well as the location for the Webster & Stevens photography studio from 1917 to 1928. The open area in front of the building was named after Times Square in New York City and was a popular gathering place. This photo shows the wide front end of the triangular Times Square Building. To the right of the doorway is the Times Automatic Baseball Player board, which gave the crowds in the square almost spontaneous coverage of the 1920 World Series and other games.

The *Seattle Times* has long since moved its headquarters to a much larger building south of Lake Union, but its old home remains part of the cityscape. The curving, elevated concrete rails in front of it are tracks for the city monorail, a limited-capacity fast transit system running from Seattle Center to Westlake Center. The Westlake Center Office Tower stands at left.

Seattle's Hotel Washington, named the Denny Hotel when it opened in 1890, sat grandly on top of Denny Hill between Second and Fourth Avenues and Stewart and Virginia Streets. The elegant building survived only until 1906, when the western part of Denny Hill was leveled. Here the hotel can be seen decorated to welcome an important visitor, possibly President Theodore Roosevelt in 1903.

The leveling of the western part of Denny Hill had a dramatic effect on the
northern edge of the downtown area, paving the way for expansion and
linking the city center with Belltown, Queen Anne Hill, and Lake Union.
The area once occupied by the hotel is now in the immediate vicinity of
Westlake Center and the Public Market.

The Belltown area of Seattle was named for William Bell, one of Seattle's first settlers. At first this mainly residential area was almost completely separated from the downtown area by Denny Hill, but by 1911 part of Denny Hill had been removed and the famous fire of 1889 had destroyed many of the homes and small business. These were replaced by the hotels and other commercial buildings seen here.

Probably taken in 1915, the photo shows the view south from Battery Street along First Avenue after the Belltown fire and the regrading project. Part of the domed wooden Bell Hotel (left) stands next door to the ornate brick Austin A. Bell Building (center).

The façade of the Bell Building, altered and modernized, still graces First Avenue, though the Bell Hotel no longer stands. Belltown maintains a semblance of its original, independent identity, but the expansion of the downtown area makes the boundary rather blurred. Two blocks west of this intersection, piers and ferry docks line the Seattle waterfront.

Cable cars were ill-suited to Seattle's steep hills so when the North Seattle Cable Railway Company began construction on the Queen Anne Avenue cable car line in 1890 the car had to be linked by cable to a 16-ton counterbalance weight. As the weight slid down the hill in its underground tunnel it pulled the cable car up. When the cable car came down the hill it hauled the weight back up to the top. This photo, taken around 1900, shows two cable cars on Queen Anne Avenue, in the area some people still call the "Counterbalance." The huge weight is underground and cannot be seen in the photo. The counterbalance system stayed in operation until 1940, when Seattle's cable cars were replaced by buses.

The cable cars are long gone in this view of Queen Anne Avenue, looking north toward the base of one of the three massive television broadcast towers that dominate the top of Queen Anne Hill. The avenue runs over the crest of the hill before jogging down the northeast slope toward Aurora Avenue and Lake Union.

This photo shows the view from Queen Anne Hill toward downtown Seattle. The Civic Auditorium and Arena, now the Seattle Opera House and Mercer Arena, stand at the corner of Mercer Street and Third Avenue North. After the partial removal of Denny Hill, Seattle was able to expand northward past Mercer Street and the city's auditorium and arena, as well as the stadium, and veterans' hall were built in what is now Seattle Center.

A view looking southwest across Seattle Center and Elliott Bay toward the Harbor Island shipyards at the mouth of the Duwamish Waterway (left background) and West Seattle (right background). The Space Needle (left) and Key Arena (pyramid-shaped roof, right) are the primary attractions of Seattle Center, though the original site for the 1962 World's Fair is undergoing a great deal of renovation and improvement.

The Space Needle, erected as the centerpiece and symbol of the 1962 World Exposition held in Seattle, nears completion in this aerial view. Cranes atop the tripod-type support structure are working to finish the disk-shaped observation deck and rotating restaurant. Standing 605 feet, the Space Needle replaced the Smith Tower as Seattle's tallest structure.

The most recognizable symbol of Seattle nearly 40 years after its construction, the Space Needle recently underwent structural maintenance. The inset clearly shows the observation platform and the famous revolving restaurant, which afford visitors all-around views of the city and its environs.

In the late 1920s Lake Union was a place of great industry. Lining its shores were a lumber mill, a brickyard, a dry dock, the city gasworks, and other manufacturing plants, many of which can be seen in this photo. Dating from around 1928 and taken from Capitol Hill it shows smoke floating above the Fremont and Ballard lumber mills. Surplus wooden warships from World War I are anchored in the middle of the lake, and a group of houseboats can be seen near the right-hand shore.

Though still supporting a number of commercial ventures, mostly along its northern shore, Lake Union now hosts a vast array of recreational vessels as well. This view from Capitol Hill looks west toward the Aurora Bridge (right center), with Queen Anne Hill on the left and Fremont and Ballard beyond. In the far background are the mountains of Washington's Olympic Peninsula.

The Aurora Bridge stretches across the Lake Washington Ship Canal. The route of its approach road from the north was controversial as, in spite of opposition, the road was built through the Aurora neighborhood and Woodland Park. This photo, taken about 1931, shows the supports of the bridge under construction. Logs float near the lumber mill at the base of the bridge.

Supplanted by the Interstate Five Ship Canal Bridge as the main north–south span, the Aurora Bridge remains one of the most heavily traveled bridges in the city. Connecting downtown and Queen Anne with the Fremont and Wallingford neighborhoods, the bridge is a critical link in Seattle's commuter traffic flow, allowing relatively easy direct access to the city from the north.

The Lake Washington Ship Canal opened for business on July 4, 1917, and the *Seattle Times* reported that on that day roads, cars, and streetcars heading for the canal were jammed with people wanting to join in the celebration. This photo shows the traffic at the south end of the Fremont Bridge on the afternoon the canal opened.

The Fremont drawbridge has recently been repainted in its distinctive blue and orange color scheme. Here we look north across it into the neighborhood along Fremont Avenue from the south side of the ship canal. The eclectic nature of Fremont's character is precisely captured by a road sign posted on this end of the span, which proclaims the area as "The Center of The Universe" and advises visitors to "turn your watch back five minutes."

Seattle's Fremont neighborhood, northwest of Lake Union, was named for John C. Fremont, the western explorer. Fremont started in the 1880s as a settlement around a sawmill and grew to a town of 5,000 before it became part of Seattle in 1891. Lake Union originally emptied into Salmon Bay through a narrow channel called the Outlet; by 1916 this had been enlarged to become part of the Lake Washington Ship Canal.

This photo shows Fremont Avenue around 1892. A sawmill stands to the right of the small wooden bridge over the Outlet. The large square brick building in the distant center of the photo is B. F. Day School, dedicated in 1892.

Downtown Fremont from the northern end of the drawbridge. Fremont Avenue runs north toward Woodland Park, site of the city's popular zoo. A block to the west of this street stands a 20-foot bronze sculpture of Lenin, purchased by a local businessman after the collapse of the Soviet Union and shipped to Seattle.

The Ballard Building was built in the 1920s by a group called the Fraternal Order of Eagles and so is sometimes called the Eagles Building. The opening of the Ballard Building marked the shift of Ballard's commercial area to Market Street. This photo shows the multi-purpose Ballard Building in 1927. It houses the Bagdad Theater, drug and department stores, and meeting rooms for the Fraternal Order of Eagles.

The Ballard Building still serves as a multi-purpose facility, housing a variety of businesses. Though shopping and tourism have become a major part of Ballard's economy, there remains a strong sense of seafaring Scandinavian heritage in the neighborhood, the legacy of its original inhabitants. Hundreds of commercial fishing vessels are moored along the wharves of the ship canal south of Market Street.

This photo shows the University Bridge under construction. Piles of lumber sit near the south end of the bridge and the northern approach hasn't been built yet. The bridge, which spans the Lake Washington Ship Canal, opened to traffic in 1919 and was the first in Seattle, perhaps in the country, to use open mesh steel decking.

This lighter construction material allowed the bridge to be wider and carry more traffic. Over the years it has also been known as the Eastlake Avenue Bridge and the Tenth Avenue Northeast Bridge.

Two distinct generations of bridge design are on show in this contemporary photograph: the University drawbridge viewed from the east, seemingly quaint when compared with the double-decked steel frame of the Interstate Five Ship Canal Bridge towering over it to the west, with the northern edge of Lake Union beyond. In all, six vehicle bridges span the waterways that divide Seattle from its northern neighborhoods and suburbs.

The Seattle Yacht Club had its first home in West Seattle but after the Lake Washington Ship Canal opened in 1919, the club built new facilities in Montlake, on Portage Bay. This gave members a sheltered place to keep their boats and access to both Lake Washington and Puget Sound. The fresh water of Portage Bay also kept destructive barnacles from growing on the boats' hulls.

In April 1930, a few days before the annual opening day, the photographer took this photo from the north end of Capitol Hill. It shows the Seattle Yacht Club, Portage Bay, and various buildings on the campus of the University of Washington.

Portage Bay retains its appeal for boaters seeking convenient moorage, and the Seattle Yacht Club is one of the region's most prestigious. Access to Puget Sound from Montlake requires transiting Lake Union and the ship canal before reaching the Hiram Chittenden Locks south of Ballard, which lower vessels to sea level for the journey out.

The high point of Seattle's Fourth of July celebration in 1917 was the opening of the Lake Washington Ship Canal, after six years of construction. In this photo spectators crowd the banks of the Montlake Cut to watch the parade of several hundred boats that passed through the new canal. This picture was taken eight years before the Montlake Bridge was built.

The southern edge of the Montlake Cut, looking east toward the Montlake drawbridge. Usually a tranquil waterway, every May the Cut is the scene of the "official" opening of the boating season, with crew regattas and festive boat parades. Vehicle and pedestrian traffic across the Cut are stopped as both the Montlake and University drawbridges are raised for several hours during this traditional event.

University Way, nicknamed "The Ave," is the business district closest to the University of Washington. University students, faculty, and staff can easily walk to the University Bookstore, restaurants, banks, and other businesses in the area. This photo shows "The Ave," with its streetcar tracks, in about 1927.

The intersection today, at the heart of the University district. With 35,000 students and a sprawling campus, the University of Washington is the dominant economic and cultural influence in the neighborhood that bears its name. The U-District and "The Ave" are renowned as centers of independent thought and behavior, carving out their own niche in Seattle's urban environment.

Left: Madison Park, at the end of the Madison Street Cable Car line, was one of Seattle's privately-developed "trolley parks." In addition to a ferry landing, it had a pavilion, a boathouse, picnic areas, piers, a promenade, and offshore bandstands with shoreline seating. This photo shows the concession area at Madison Park in about 1910. On that day, hungry or thirsty visitors could buy candy, fruit, and a variety of drinks.

Right: Looking north along the shore of Lake Washington at Madison Park. The waters of the lake are very popular with residents during the summer months, attracting droves of boaters and beachgoers; the vast majority of boat traffic on the lake is recreational. Lake Washington also hosts the famous hydroplane races during the Seafair festival in August.

In the 1890s, John McGilvra developed Madison Park at the end of his
trolley line. Around 1900, Seattleites could swim, rent boats, and buy
refreshments at the Eagle Bath House and Boat House. The park also had
piers, bandstands, gardens, a dance pavilion, and a promenade. This photo,
taken around 1900, shows the Eagle Bath and Boat House and the paths
through the gardens.

Playground equipment and shade trees emphasize Madison Park's current role as a popular gathering place for families. The residential neighborhoods around the park — along Lake Washington Boulevard and East Madison Street, and south of the nearby University of Washington Arboretum — are noted for their affluence.

Leschi Park, on the shore of Lake Washington, was a popular place for Seattle's city-dwellers to go for recreation. Many people caught a cable car at Pioneer Square and rode to the park along Yesler Way. In this photo, taken around 1911, people sit or stroll in the park while others relax in their rented canoes. The men and women may seem formally dressed by modern standards, but this would have been typical clothing for a summer outing in 1911.

An assortment of pleasure craft moored at the marina near Leschi Park, with Lake Washington and the communities of Bellevue and Kirkland in the background. During the Seafair festival, the popular aerobatic demonstrations by the U.S. Navy's "Blue Angels" flying team over the lake draw thousands of spectators to viewpoints like Leschi Park.

This photo looks to the east over the Lake Washington Floating Bridge toward Mercer Island. Named in memory of Lacey V. Murrow, former head of the state's highway department, work on the world's first large-scale floating bridge began in the late 1930s, and it opened for traffic on July 2, 1940. The concrete roadway from Seattle to the eastern shore of Lake Washington floats on pontoons which are anchored to the lake bottom.

The bridge helped the World War II effort by shortening the commute between Seattle's eastern suburbs and the downtown industrial area. It also helped lead to the expansion of the suburbs.

A second floating bridge (left) was added in 1990 to the original to ease the burden created by the heavy traffic on Interstate 90. These are currently two of the four longest floating spans in the United States. The longest is just a few miles to the north, also on Lake Washington: the Evergreen Point Bridge, supporting State Route 520 and connecting Seattle to the communities of Bellevue, Kirkland, and Redmond on the east side of the lake.

Three Sisters of Providence arrived in Seattle from Vancouver, Washington, in May 1877 to manage the King County Poor Farm on the Duwamish River. In May 1878 the sisters purchased and remodeled a house at Fifth Avenue and Madison, and established the first Providence Hospital. The group built a second, larger hospital in several phases, beginning in 1882.

This photo, taken around 1904, shows Providence Hospital's second building, on Fifth Avenue between Madison and Spring Streets. This site, just uphill from the Public Library (still a vacant lot in this photo), is now occupied by the U.S. District Court. The old wooden hospital building was demolished in 1914, after Providence Hospital moved to its current location at Seventeenth Avenue and Jefferson Street.

The western face of the old Providence building today, in its guise as the U.S.
District Court. This view was taken from the west side of Fifth Avenue,
where the main branch of the Seattle Public Library now stands. At right is
the flank of the Bank of America Fifth Avenue Plaza, completed in 1981.

St. James Cathedral was built to celebrate the move of the Roman Catholic archdiocese from Vancouver, Washington, to Seattle. The first stone was laid in 1905, and the 14,000-seat building opened two years later. Situated on the corner of Ninth Avenue and Marion Street on First Hill, the building and its tall towers can still be seen from many parts of downtown Seattle.

The cathedral today marks the proverbial center of Roman Catholicism in the region. Just to the east of St. James is O'Dea High School, an all-boys institution that ranks among Seattle's most respected preparatory academies, while the campus of Seattle University, a Jesuit school dating back to 1891, lies about half of a mile east of O'Dea.

Seattle's First Hill got its name because it was the closest hill to the downtown area. This photo shows the northeast corner of Minor Avenue and Columbia Street in the 1890s. The John Sanderson family lived in the large home on the corner and other early residents in the area included the Dennys, Terrys, Minors, Burkes, and other members of Seattle's social elite. From their large homes on the hillside they could look down across the growing city where they made their living. The neighborhood began to change around 1908, when Swedish and Cabrini Hospitals bought property there.

The corner of Minor and Columbia is now at the heart of the large Swedish Medical Center complex on First Hill; construction on the facility continues, with more buildings being added. Swedish is just one of four major hospitals that now dominate the area around First Hill: the others include Providence, Harborview, and Virginia Mason.

Left: This photo shows the Hotel Sorrento in about 1912. By this date a number of hotels had been built just outside Seattle's downtown area for people traveling on business or pleasure. The Hotel Sorrento, which advertised itself as "a hotel in the heart of things," opened on First Hill in 1908. It had Seattle's first rooftop restaurant, a roof garden, and scenic views of the city, the bay, and the mountains.

Right: The Sorrento remains on the edge of downtown, separated from the city center by the artificial boundary created by Interstate Five. Its brick construction and elegant architecture stand in stark contrast to the more modern, streamlined appearance of Seattle's later hotels, several of which are visible from the Sorrento's upper floors.

Above: In the early 1900s the Olmsted Brothers firm of landscape designers submitted a plan for Volunteer Park to the city of Seattle. It included curving roads and formal gardens. A water tower was also built in 1906, and a conservatory added in 1912. This photo shows the reservoir, small lily ponds, gardens, and a long pavilion with a bandstand at the center. The gardens are gone now, the Seattle Asian Art Museum standing where the pavilion was.

Inset: Three girls sit on the lawn enjoying the late afternoon sun in Seattle's Volunteer Park, named in honor of the men who served in the 1898 Spanish–American War. The plan was designed to harmonize with surrounding Capitol Hill neighborhood. This photo shows an area of Volunteer Park with rose gardens, lawns, winding paths, and a water tower with an observation area.

Above: Volunteer Park's central thoroughfare, flanked by heavy tree cover, with part of the Seattle Asian Art Museum visible on the right. The Capitol Hill neighborhood combines tranquil foliage and impressive rows of stately homes with the vibrant activity along Broadway, which runs east of Volunteer Park.

Inset: Another view of Volunteer Park today. Roughly the geographic center of the Capitol Hill neighborhood, northwest of downtown, and bordered to the north by Lake View Cemetery and ringed by some of the city's oldest residential areas, the park is one of a series of "green spots" that dot the hills between Lake Union and Lake Washington.

This photo shows St. Mark's Cathedral shortly before its 1931 dedication. Construction of the cathedral began on Capitol Hill during the 1920s and the original plans called for a huge, Gothic-style structure. However, funding was cut back drastically during the Great Depression and only the central part of the cathedral was eventually built. St. Mark's still serves as the cathedral for Episcopalians in the northwest.

Today St. Mark's is one of Seattle's most visible churches, looming above the bustling traffic on Interstate Five from its perch atop Capitol Hill. At night, the western face of the cathedral is illuminated by powerful floodlights, creating a beautiful, haunting beacon of religious architecture that can be seen from many miles away on a clear evening.

In 1942 construction started on a new international airport between Seattle and Tacoma. The new airport, dubbed SeaTac, was formally dedicated on July 9, 1949. It cost $11 million and opened free of debt. United Airlines, Northwest Airlines, Pan American World Airways, and Western Airlines started their regular passenger service at SeaTac on the day of the dedication. This July 1949 photo shows the front of the Seattle–Tacoma International Airport passenger terminal during the opening day air show. Port of Seattle officials estimated that 30,000 people attended the opening ceremonies to tour the new airport and inspect the planes.

SeaTac International now ranks in the top forty among the world's airports in both passengers and cargo. Briefly renamed in the 1980s to honor the late Washington senator Henry M. Jackson, the change was unpopular, and the airport's original name was soon restored. Debate over the location of a possible third runway at SeaTac is a volatile issue in the area, with landowners around the airport generally disapproving of the proposal.

In 1900, Anders Wilse stood on top of Denny Hill to take this photo of downtown Seattle, Beacon Hill, and Mt. Rainier. At that time, much of Beacon Hill was still wooded and Mt. Rainier seems to float in the distance. The Pioneer Square area is in the lower right of the photograph.

The icy, impassive northern flank of Mt. Rainier today, seemingly unchanged a century later. The crown jewel of the Cascade range, residents marvel at its beauty but watch it with a wary eye: the violent eruption of her southerly sister, Mt. St. Helens, in 1980 shook the region from its rather casual attitude about the volcanic nature of the nearby mountains.

INDEX